BOB DYLAN
MODERN TIMES

AMSCO PUBLICATIONS
part of The Music Sales Group
New York/London/Paris/Sydney/Copenhagen/Berlin/Tokyo/Madrid

Cover photo: "Taxi, New York at Night" © Ted Croner Estate/
Courtesy of Howard Greenburg Gallery, New York
Additional photography by Kevin Mazur
Art Direction by Geoff Gans
Arrangements for publication by David Pearl
Project Editor: David Bradley

This book published 2006 by Amsco Publications,
A Division of Music Sales Corporation, New York

Order No. AM 986931
ISBN-10: 0.8256.3497-0
ISBN-13: 978.0.8256.3497.0

Exclusive Distributors:
Music Sales Corporation
257 Park Avenue South, New York, NY 10010 USA
Music Sales Limited
14-15 Berners Street, London W1T 3LJ England
Music Sales Pty. Limited
120 Rothschild Street, Rosebery, Sydney, NSW 2018, Australia

Printed in the United States of America

THUNDER ON THE MOUNTAIN

Words and Music by Bob Dylan

1. Thun - der on the moun-tain, fires on the moon___ There's a ruck - us in the al - ley and the

2. - 16. *See additional lyrics*

sun will be here soon   To - day's the day, gon - na grab my trom - bone and

blow_____   Well, there's hot_____ stuff here_____ and it's

1. - 15.

ev' - ry - where I go_____   2. I was think - in' 'bout

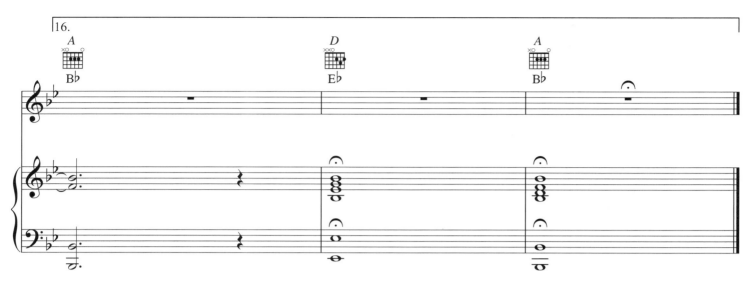

Additional lyrics

2. I was thinkin' 'bout Alicia Keys, couldn't keep from crying
   When she was born in Hell's Kitchen, I was living down the line
   I'm wondering where in the world Alicia Keys could be
   I been looking for her even clear through Tennessee

3. Feel like my soul is beginning to expand
   Look into my heart and you will sort of understand
   You brought me here, now you're trying to run me away
   The writing's on the wall, come read it, come see what it say

4. *Instrumental*

5. Thunder on the mountain, rolling like a drum
   Gonna sleep over there, that's where the music coming from
   I don't need any guide, I already know the way
   Remember this, I'm your servant both night and day

6. The pistols are poppin' and the power is down
   I'd like to try somethin' but I'm so far from town
   The sun keeps shinin' and the North Wind keeps picking up speed
   Gonna forget about myself for a while, gonna go out and see what others need

7. I've been sitting down studying the art of love
   I think it will fit me like a glove
   I want some real good woman to do just what I say
   Everybody got to wonder what's the matter with this cruel world today

8. *Instrumental*

9. Thunder on the mountain rolling to the ground
   Gonna get up in the morning walk the hard road down
   Some sweet day I'll stand beside my king
   I wouldn't betray your love or any other thing

10. Gonna raise me an army, some tough sons of bitches
    I'll recruit my army from the orphanages
    I been to St. Herman's church and I've said my religious vows
    I've sucked the milk out of a thousand cows

11. I got the porkchops, she got the pie
    She ain't no angel and neither am I
    Shame on your greed, shame on your wicked schemes
    I'll say this, I don't give a damn about your dreams

12. *Instrumental*

13. Thunder on the mountain heavy as can be
    Mean old twister bearing down on me
    All the ladies of Washington scrambling to get out of town
    Looks like something bad gonna happen, better roll your airplane down

14. Everybody's going and I want to go too
    Don't wanna take a chance with somebody new
    I did all I could and I did it right there and then
    I've already confessed—no need to confess again

15. Gonna make a lot of money, gonna go up north
    I'll plant and I'll harvest what the earth brings forth
    The hammer's on the table, the pitchfork's on the shelf
    For the love of God, you ought to take pity on yourself

16. *Instrumental*

SPIRIT ON THE WATER

Words and Music by Bob Dylan

I'd for - got-ten a-bout you____ Then you turned up a-gain____

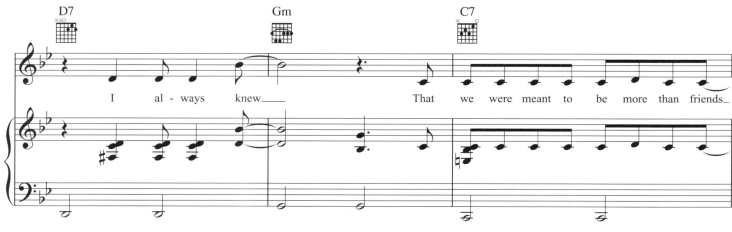

I al - ways knew____ That we were meant to be more than friends____

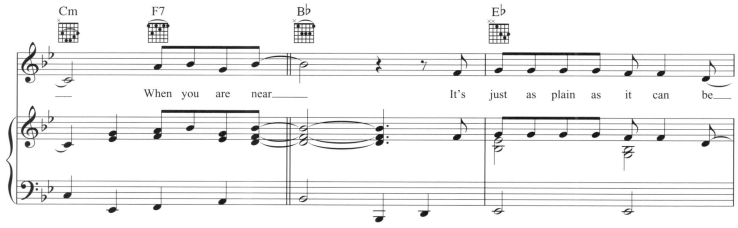

When you are near____ It's just as plain as it can be____

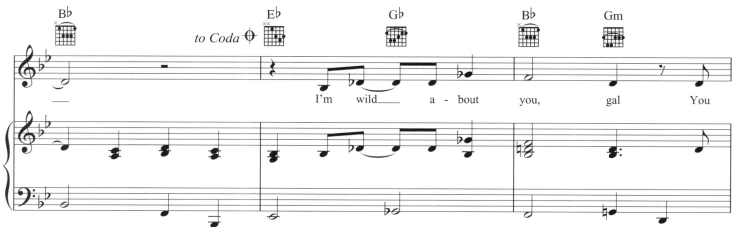

to Coda I'm wild____ a - bout you, gal You

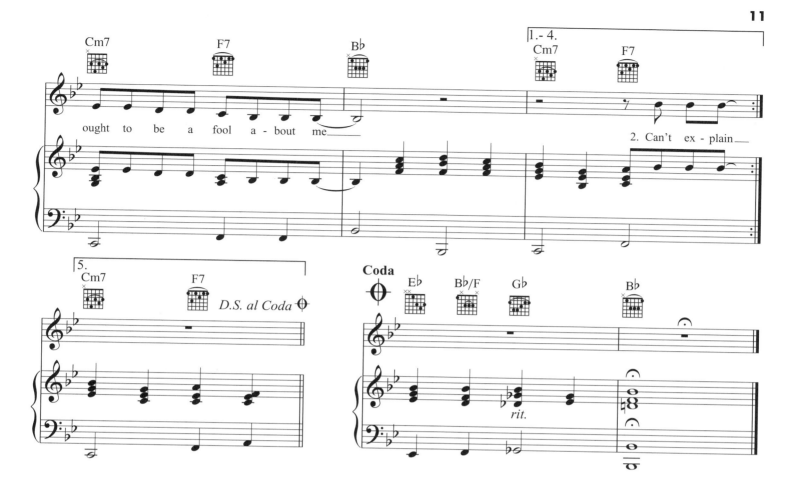

Additional lyrics

2. Can't explain
   The sources of this hidden pain
   You burned your way into my heart
   You got the key to my brain

   I've been trampling through mud
   Praying to the powers above
   I'm sweating blood
   You got a face that begs for love

   Life without you
   Doesn't mean a thing to me
   If I can't have you,
   I'll throw my love into the deep blue sea

   Sometimes I wonder
   Why you can't treat me right
   You do good all day
   Then you do wrong all night

3. When you're with me
   I'm a thousand times happier
      than I could ever say
   What does it matter
   What price I pay

   They brag about your sugar
   Brag about it all over town
   Put some sugar in my bowl
   I feel like laying down

   I'm pale as a ghost
   Holding a blossom on a stem
   You ever see a ghost? No
   But you have heard of them

   I see you there
   I'm blinded by the colors I see
   I take good care
   Of what belongs to me

4. I hear your name
   Ringing up and down the line
   I'm saying it plain
   These ties are strong enough to bind

   Your sweet voice
   Calls out from some old familiar shrine
   I got no choice
   Can't believe these things would ever
      fade from your mind

      I could live forever
      With you perfectly
      You don't ever
      Have to make a fuss over me

   From East to West
   Ever since the world began
   I only mean it for the best
   I want to be with you any way I can

5. I been in a brawl
   Now I'm feeling the wall
   I'm going away baby
   I won't be back 'til fall

   High on the hill
   You can carry all my thoughts with you
   You've numbed my will
   This love could tear me in two

      I wanna be with you in paradise
      And it seems so unfair
      I can't go to paradise no more
      I killed a man back there

   You think I'm over the hill
   You think I'm past my prime
   Let me see what you got
   We can have a whoppin' good time

6. *Instrumental*

ROLLIN' AND TUMBLIN'

Words and Music by Bob Dylan

Fast 2-beat

Guitar capo 1st fret

rolled and I tum-bled, I cried the whole night long___

2. - 13. *See additional lyrics*

rolled and I tum-bled, I____ cried the whole____ night long____

1. - 12.

Woke up this morn-in', I must have bet my mon-ey____ wrong____

2. I got

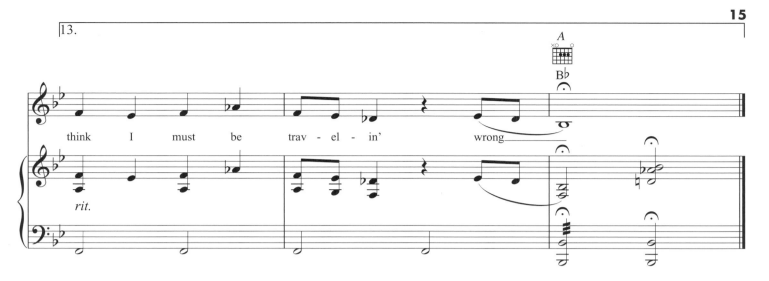

think   I   must   be   trav - el - in'   wrong

rit.

Additional lyrics

2. I got troubles so hard, I can't stand the strain
    I got troubles so hard, I just can't stand the strain
    Some young lazy slut has charmed away my brains

3. The landscape is glowin', gleamin' in the golden light of day
    The landscape is glowin', gleamin' in the gold light of day
    I ain't holding nothin' back now,
        I ain't standin' in anybody's way

4. Well, I did all I know just to keep you off my mind
    Well, I did all I know just to keep you off my mind
    Well, I paid and I paid and my sufferin' heart
        is always on the line

5. Well, I get up in the dawn and I go down
        and lay in the shade
    I get up in the dawn and I go down and lay in the shade
    I ain't nobody's house boy, I ain't nobody's
        well-trained maid

6. I'm flat-out spent, this woman been drivin' me to tears
    I'm flat-out spent, this woman she been drivin' me to tears
    This woman so crazy, I swear I ain't gonna touch
        another one for years

7. *Instrumental*

8. Well, the warm weather is comin' and the buds are on the vine
    The warm weather's comin', the buds are on the vine
    Ain't nothing more depressing as trying to
        satisfy this woman of mine

9. I got up this mornin', saw the rising sun return
    Well, I got up this mornin', seen the rising sun return
    Sooner or later you too shall burn

10. *Instrumental*

11. The night's filled with shadows,
        the years are filled with early doom
    The night's filled with shadows,
        the years are filled with early doom
    I've been conjuring up all these long-dead souls
        from their crumblin' tombs

12. Let's forgive each other darlin',
        let's go down to the greenwood glen
    Let's forgive each other darlin',
        let's go down to the greenwood glen
    Let's put our heads together,
        let's put old matters to an end

13. Now I rolled and I tumbled and I cried
        the whole night long
    Ah, I rolled and I tumbled, I cried
        the whole night long
    I woke up this morning, I think I must
        be travelin' wrong

WHEN THE DEAL GOES DOWN

Words and Music by Bob Dylan

Additional lyrics

2. We eat and we drink, we feel and we think
   Far down the street we stray
   I laugh and I cry and I'm haunted by
   Things I never meant nor wished to say
   The midnight rain follows the train
   We all wear the same thorny crown
   Soul to soul, our shadows roll
   And I'll be with you when the deal goes down

3. The moon gives light and shines by night
   I scarcely feel the glow
   We learn to live and then we forgive
   O'er the road we're bound to go
   More frailer than the flowers, these precious hours
   That keep us so tightly bound
   You come to my eyes like a vision from the skies
   And I'll be with you when the deal goes down

4. I picked up a rose and it poked through my clothes
   I followed the winding stream
   I heard a deafening noise, I felt transient joys
   I know they're not what they seem
   In this earthly domain, full of disappointment and pain
   You'll never see me frown
   I owe my heart to you, and that's sayin' it true
   And I'll be with you when the deal goes down

SOMEDAY BABY
Words and Music by Bob Dylan

1. I don't care__ what you do,__
2. - 13. *See additional lyrics*

I don't care__ what you say__   I don't care__ where you go__

or how long_____ you stay   Some - day__ ba-

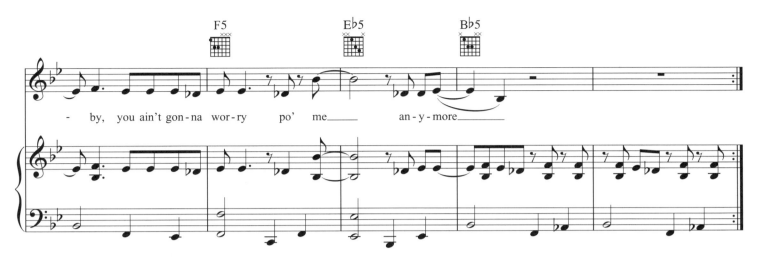

- by, you ain't gon-na wor-ry po' me_____ an-y-more_____

Additional lyrics

2. Well you take my money and you turn me out
   You fill me up with nothin' but self-doubt
   Someday baby, you ain't gonna worry po' me
   anymore

3. When I was young, driving was my crave
   You drive me so hard, almost to the grave
   Someday baby, you ain't gonna worry po' me
   anymore

4. *Instrumental*

5. I'm so hard pressed, my mind tied up in knots
   I keep recycling the same old thoughts
   Someday baby, you ain't gonna worry po' me
   anymore

6. So many good things in life that I overlooked
   I don't know what to do now, you got me
   so hooked
   Someday baby, you ain't gonna worry po' me
   anymore

7. *Instrumental*

8. Well, I don't want to brag, but I'm gonna ring your
   neck
   When all else fails I'll make it a matter of self-respect
   Someday baby, you ain't gonna worry po' me
   anymore

9. *Instrumental*

10. You can take your clothes put 'm in a sack
    You goin' down the road, baby and you can't
    come back
    Someday baby, you ain't gonna worry po' me
    anymore

11. I try to be friendly, I try to be kind
    Now I'm gonna drive you from your home,
    just like I was driven from mine
    Someday baby, you ain't gonna worry po' me
    anymore

12. Living this way ain't a natural thing to do
    Why was I born to love you?
    Someday baby, you ain't gonna worry po' me
    anymore

13. *Instrumental (fade)*

WORKINGMAN'S BLUES #2
Words and Music by Bob Dylan

lis - ten - in' to the steel rails___ hum   Got both eyes___ tight shut   Just

sit - ting here trying to keep the hun - ger from   Creep -ing its way in - to my gut___

Chorus

Meet me at the bot - tom, don't lag be - hind___   Bring me my boots and shoes   You can

hang back or fight your best on___ the front line   Sing a lit - tle bit of these work-ing-man's   blues___

2. Now, I'm

Additional lyrics

2. Now, I'm sailin' on back, ready for the long haul
   Tossed by the winds and the seas
   I'll drag 'em all down to hell and I'll stand 'em
     at the wall
   I'll sell 'em to their enemies
   I'm tryin' to feed my soul with thought
   Gonna sleep off the rest of the day
   Sometimes no one wants what we got
   Sometimes you can't give it away

   Now the place is ringed with countless foes
   Some of them may be deaf and dumb
   No man, no woman knows
   The hour that sorrow will come
   In the dark I hear the night birds call
   I can hear a lover's breath
   I sleep in the kitchen with my feet in the hall
   Sleep is like a temporary death

   (Chorus)

3. Well, they burned my barn, they stole my horse
   I can't save a dime
   I got to be careful, I don't want to be forced
   Into a life of continual crime
   I can see for myself that the sun is sinking
   How I wish you were here to see
   Tell me now, am I wrong in thinking
   That you have forgotten me?

   Now they worry and they hurry and they fuss
     and they fret
   They waste your nights and days
   Them I will forget
   But you I'll remember always
   Old memories of you to me have clung
   You've wounded me with words
   Gonna have to straighten out your tongue
   It's all true, everything you have heard

   (Chorus)

4. In you, my friend, I find no blame
   Wanna look in my eyes, please do
   No one can ever claim
   That I took up arms against you
   All across the peaceful sacred fields
   They will lay you low
   They'll break your horns and slash
     you with steel
   I say it so it must be so

   Now I'm down on my luck and I'm
     black and blue
   Gonna give you another chance
   I'm all alone and I'm expecting you
   To lead me off in a cheerful dance
   Got a brand new suit and a brand new wife
   I can live on rice and beans
   Some people never worked a day in their life
   Don't know what work even means

   (Chorus)

5. Instrumental (fade)

BEYOND THE HORIZON

Words and Music by Bob Dylan

Moderately, with a swing

1. Be-yond the ho-ri-zon, be-hind the sun

2.-4. *See additional lyrics*

At the end of the rain-bow life has on-ly be-gun

In the long hours of twi-light 'neath the star-dust a-bove

Love waits for - ev - er   for one and for all_____

2. Be - yond the ho - ri -

3., 4. Be - yond the ho - ri -

rit.

Additional lyrics

2. Beyond the horizon across the divide
   'Round about midnight, we'll be on the same side
   Down in the valley the water runs cold
   Beyond the horizon someone prayed for your soul

   I'm touched with desire
   What don't I do?
   I'll throw the logs on the fire
   I'll build my world around you

   Beyond the horizon, at the end of the game
   Every step that you take, I'm walking the same

3. Beyond the horizon the night winds blow
   The theme of a melody from many moons ago
   The bells of St. Mary, how sweetly they chime
   Beyond the horizon I found you just in time

   It's dark and it's dreary
   I ponder in vain
   I'm weakened, I'm weary
   My repentance is plain

   Beyond the horizon o'er the treacherous sea
   I still can't believe that you've set aside your love for me

4. Beyond the horizon, 'neath crimson skies
   In the soft light of morning I'll follow you with my eyes
   Through countries and kingdoms and temples of stone
   Beyond the horizon right down to the bone

   It's late in the season
   Never knew, never cared
   Whatever the reason
   Someone's life has been spared

   Beyond the horizon the sky is so blue
   I've got more than a lifetime to live lovin' you

THE LEVEE'S GONNA BREAK

Words and Music by Bob Dylan

1. If it keep on rain-in' the lev-ee gon-na break   If it
2. - 19. *See additional lyrics*

keep on rain-in' the lev-ee gon-na break   Ev'-ry-

bod-y say-ing this is a day— on-ly The Lord could make   2. Well I

Additional lyrics

2. Well I worked on the levee Mama, both night and day
   Well I worked on the levee Mama, both night and day
   I got to the river and I threw my clothes away

3. I paid my time and now I'm as good as new
   I paid my time and now I'm as good as new
   They can't take me back, not unless I want them to

4. If it keep on rainin' the levee gonna break
   If it keep on rainin' the levee gonna break
   Some of these people gonna strip you of all they can take

5. *Instrumental*

6. I can't stop here, I ain't ready to unload
   I can't stop here, I ain't ready to unload
   Riches and salvation can be waiting
     behind the next bend in the road

7. I picked you up from the gutter and this is the thanks I get
   I picked you up from the gutter and this is the thanks I get
   You say you want me to quit ya, I told you no, not just yet

8. I look in your eyes, I see nobody else but me
   I look in your eyes, I see nobody other than me
   I see all that I am and all I hope to be

9. If it keep on rainin' the levee gonna break
   If it keep on rainin' the levee gonna break
   Some of these people don't know which road to take

10. *Instrumental*

11. When I'm with you I forget I was ever blue
    When I'm with you I forget I was ever blue
    Without you there's no meaning in anything I do

12. Some people on the road carrying everything that they own
    Some people on the road carrying everything that they own
    Some people got barely enough skin to cover their bones

13. Put on your cat clothes, Mama, put on your evening dress
    Put on your cat clothes, Mama, put on your evening dress
    A few more years of hard work then there'll be
      a thousand years of happiness

14. If it keep on rainin' the levee gonna break
    If it keep on rainin' the levee gonna break
    I tried to get you to love me, but I won't repeat that mistake

15. *Instrumental*

16. If it keep on rainin' the levee gonna break
    If it keep on rainin' the levee gonna break
    Plenty of cheap stuff out there still around to take

17. I woke up this morning, butter and eggs in my bed
    I woke up this morning, butter and eggs in my bed
    I ain't got enough room to even raise my head

18. Come back, baby, say we never more will part
    Come back, baby, say we never more will part
    Don't be stranger without a brain or heart

19. If it keep on rainin' the levee gonna break
    If it keep on rainin' the levee gonna break
    Some people still sleepin', some people are wide awake

AIN'T TALKIN'
Words and Music by Bob Dylan

I walked out to-night___ in the mys-tic gar-den   The

2. - 8. *See additional lyrics*

1. As

one on earth would ev-er know 2. They say plague

The

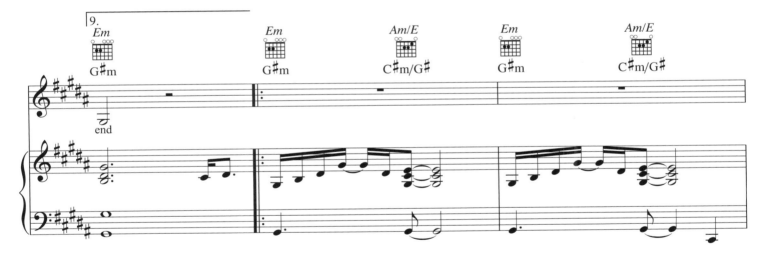

end

Additional lyrics

2. They say prayer has the power to help,
   So pray from the mother
   In the human heart an evil spirit can dwell
   I'm trying to love my neighbor and do good unto others
   But oh, mother, things ain't going well

   Chorus:
   Ain't talkin', just walkin'
   I'll burn that bridge before you can cross
   Heart burnin', still yearnin'
   There'll be no mercy for you once you've lost

3. Now I'm all worn down by weepin'
   My eyes are filled with tears, my lips are dry
   If I catch my opponents ever sleepin'
   I'll just slaughter them where they lie

   Chorus:
   Ain't talkin', just walkin'
   Through the world mysterious and vague
   Heart burnin', still yearnin'
   Walkin' through the cities of the plague

4. The whole world is filled with speculation
   The whole wide world which people say is round
   They will tear your mind away from contemplation
   They will jump on your misfortune when you're down

   Chorus:
   Ain't talkin', just walkin'
   Eatin' hog-eyed grease in hog-eyed town
   Heart burnin'—still yearnin'
   Someday you'll be glad to have me around

5. They will crush you with wealth and power
   Every waking moment you could crack
   I'll make the most of one last extra hour
   I'll avenge my father's death then I'll step back

   Chorus:
   Ain't talkin', just walkin'
   Hand me down my walkin' cane
   Heart burnin', still yearnin'
   Got to get you out of my miserable brain

6. All my loyal and my much-loved companions
   They approve of me and share my code
   I practice a faith that's been long abandoned
   Ain't no altars on this long and lonesome road

   Chorus:
   Ain't talkin', just walkin'
   My mule is sick, my horse is blind
   Heart burnin', still yearnin'
   Thinkin' 'bout that gal I left behind

7. It's bright in the heavens and the wheels are flying
   Fame and honor never seem to fade
   The fire's gone out but the light is never dying
   Who says I can't get heavenly aid?

   Chorus:
   Ain't talkin', just walkin'
   Carrying a dead man's shield
   Heart burnin', still yearnin'
   Walkin' with a toothache in my heel

8. The suffering is unending
   Every nook and cranny has its tears
   I'm not playing, I'm not pretending
   I'm not nursing any superfluous fears

   Chorus:
   Ain't talkin', just walkin'
   Walkin' ever since the other night
   Heart burnin', still yearnin'
   Walkin' 'til I'm clean out of sight

9. As I walked out in the mystic garden
   On a hot summer day, hot summer lawn
   Excuse me, ma'am I beg your pardon
   There's no one here, the gardener is gone

   Chorus:
   Ain't talkin', just walkin'
   Up the road around the bend
   Heart burnin', still yearnin'
   In the last outback, at the world's end

NETTIE MOORE
Words and Music by Bob Dylan

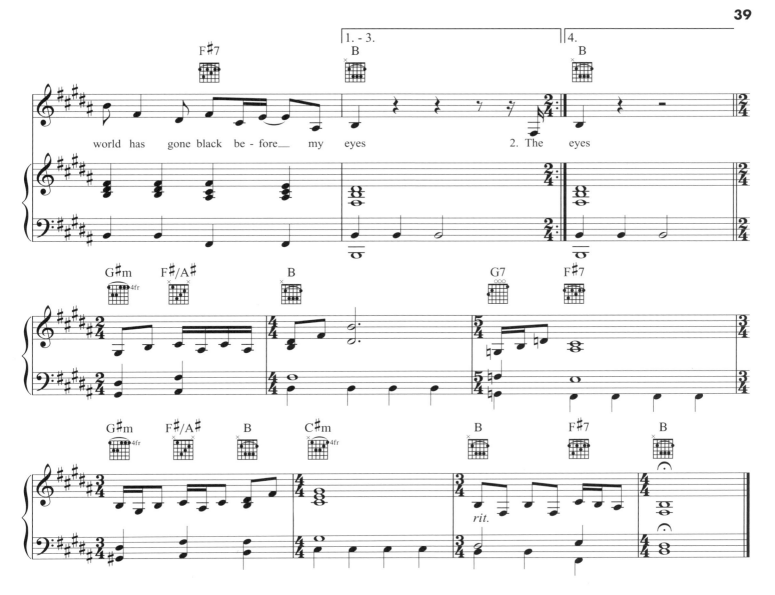

Additional lyrics

2. The world of research has gone berserk
   Too much paperwork
   Albert's in the graveyard, Frankie's raising hell
   I'm beginning to believe what the scriptures tell

   I'm going where the Southern crosses the Yellow Dog
   Get away from these demagogues
   And these bad luck women stick like glue
   It's either one or the other or neither of the two

   She says, "look out, daddy, don't want you to tear your pants.
   You can get wrecked in this dance."
   They say whiskey will kill ya, but I don't think it will
   I'm riding with you to the top of the hill

   (Chorus)

3. Don't know why my baby never looked so good before
   I don't have to wonder no more
   She been cooking all day and it's gonna take me all night
   I can't eat all that stuff in a single bite

   The Judge is coming in, everybody rise
   Lift up your eyes
   You can do what you please, you don't need my advice
   Before you call me any dirty names you better think twice

   Getting light outside, the temperature dropped
   I think the rain has stopped
   I'm going to make you come to grips with fate
   When I'm through with you, you'll learn to keep your business straight

   (Chorus)

4. The bright spark of the steady lights
   Has dimmed my sights
   When you're around all my grief gives 'way
   A lifetime with you is like some heavenly day

   Everything I've ever known to be right has proven wrong
   I'll be drifting along
   The woman I'm lovin', she rules my heart
   No knife could ever cut our love apart

   Today I'll stand in faith and raise
   The voice of praise
   The sun is strong, I'm standing in the light
   I wish to God that it were night

   (Chorus)